THE KNOTSMAN
Math Jones

ARACHNE PRESS

First published in UK 2019 by Arachne Press Limited
100 Grierson Road, London SE23 1NX
www.arachnepress.com
© Math Jones 2019
ISBN: 978-1-909208-73-5

Thanks to Muireann Grealy for her proofing.

Printed on wood-free paper in the UK by TJ International, Padstow.

THE KNOTSMAN

MATH JONES

Contents

The Last Knotsman

Apprenticeship

Loose Threads

Journeyman

Master

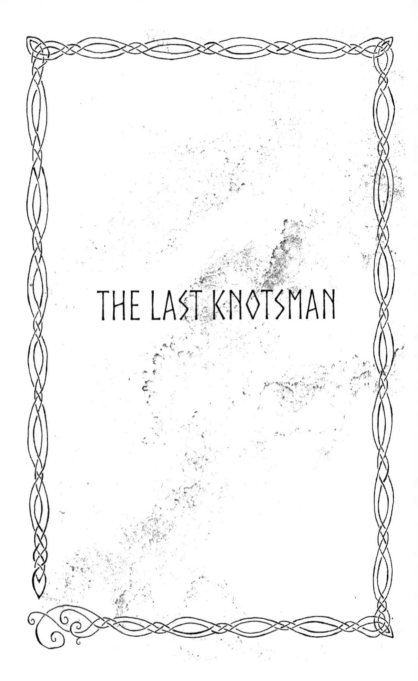

THE LAST KNOTSMAN

A True Historie of the Last Knotsman

D'ye hear the Knotsman came our way,
His tugs and picker in his case,
Calling around the market-place,
With 'is *Any strings fer me t'day?*

Did ye see the knots upon his face,
The lines and hitches tightly bound;
And trailing, like a tethered hound,
The story of his sharp disgrace:

A tale of scandal going round
Of lovers, closely knit, against
Their parents' wishes, hard, incensed,
Unless the 'trothing-rope be found,

And so the Knotsman's search commenced,
With heavy promises to find
The heart-string-join, and so unbind
The love-knot from their bloods condensed.

He spied the matted threads behind
The upper bedroom's linen-chest,
And at the mothers' fierce behest,
Began his loosing-work unkind.

The younger felt, within his breast,
The first cord of his heart untie,
And speaking to his lover's eye,
Awoke him from his joyful rest.

I say we must the world deny,
Before the hitches of our heart
Are by the Knotsman eased apart.
The river took them both to die.

Arrested for his 'devil's art',
Imprisoned by the New Belief,
All stoked by fathers' rage and grief,
The Knotsman felt the judge's dart,

But slipped his bindings, sought relief,
Escaping to our neighbour town,
Was by the constable put down
To hang from gallows on the heath.

A hangman came, of great renown,
To raise the beam and tie the noose,
A slip-knot two-step to induce,
And take the parents' silver crown.

No rope would suffer such misuse
To cause the cunning Knotsman pain,
But showed the gallows-man disdain:
The loops and hitches set him loose;

The hangman tied his rope in vain,
As through the crowd the Knotsman slipped,
Not ever by a binding gripped,
Nor never to be seen again.

The Knotsman's Apprentice

The Knottyman came to the backdoor. 'A 'strings fer me?'
Mother would turn him away, but I pulled at her sleeve. Sissy
said, 'Miss Jemima, M'm?'

He searched the linen-chests, then the boot-room; he examined
curtains, the spinning, even candle sconces. Shabby beside our
bright things. A walking shadow, quiet around Jemima's bed.

He brought three knots to the parlour: a leather cord in father's
breeches, his best. A silken from mother's undergown. She
blushed. And my bowstring, a toy left unused. All snagged and
knotted beyond untying.

Mother tutted, agreed to his 'penny a 'not'.

He let me watch, took the leather and pulled his blade. 'Ni'
t' cut, lad, nay. Niv'r t' cut'. Tight skin on bone and sinew
worked. I watched. He pushed the cords, not pulling, blew on
them, tapped, eased the loops. Soon it was free. Father stormed
into the house, shouting for mother!

He worked the silk, 'Clen han's, d'n't mith'r'. I saw him tease
the knot, split it in two, draw them apart, unbind them one
at a time. Mother was screaming upstairs. I stood. His hand
stilled me.

He took my bowstring, winked, working fingers, picking, pushing, rolling, teasing. Mother came down. Flushed, smiling. Father followed, not scowling, happy. He put coin on the table: a shilling! He took her hand.

A rush of cannonballs lurched in my stomach. Gunpowder and muskets. I stood, walking through a cavalry charge, embraced them.

The Knotsman went, leaving breeches, chemise and a new-strung, toy bow.

'Jemima, M'm! She's worse!'

She was burning, covers thrown, Sissy mopping her down. Father knelt to pray, mother sobbed.

I saw it. A single, light and crinkled thread, limp from the hem of her nightgown. Clearing my eyes, I sat at her feet. Took up the knot. Examined the thread, and picked at the first loop.

The Knotsman

Being notes and researches into the itinerant class and here recorded by the gentleman and antiquarian, Mr E., since vanished.

Knotsman – *an itinerant, a cunning man, claiming to solve the ills of a household by the unpicking of knots found within the dwelling or demesne.*

> *A' strings? A' strings?*
> *A' strings for me t' loose t'day?*

In the throng of the marketplace today,
I saw a creature sat alone, a seeming crow,
The Knotsman as he's known. I asked
If I might watch his work, write it down.
A scribbler, are ye? he replied. A gentleman, I;
A poet also, making knots of words.
I weave with rhymes and sounds.
He farted then. *Aye, so. Jus' not when I'm aroun'.*

His fingers catch the smallest fibre; just a touch,
To let it know he knows it's there;
A gentle roll to feel the threads
Within a thread, remind them each,
The twists and twills, what it feels like to be free;
Teasing, working out the strand within the tightened loop,
Pulls it clear to loose the one that's trapped beneath.

> *Take the weight away, y' see,*
> *Cup it gentle, let it ease,*
> *Stroke it, roll it, take b'th ends,*
> *Work t'ward the middle, t' the first entangle, born from kinks*
> *An' left t' curl. Mind the snarl! Purls an' stitches are my foemen!*

'Nitting gran'sires, look away! I'll throw your work,
Yer warm work, all dropped upon the stones…

                                    he grins.

A tiny tug against the strain, then round to push, then tug again
    the other way,
Enlarge the loop, leave it hanging, bring the body through the
    mouth;

Niver wet it: niver let it swell, nor too much dry,
Snappin' strings is worse than 'Ell –

With a nail, and a pin, and a close-to eye;
His pickers, teasers, hangers by;
Know the tug that will not tighten;
Know the route, the loops, the trouble takes:

    {The Hare Loop, the River Loop, the Strangle-Grip,
    The Key Thread, the Loom Weight, the Fawn and Jib
    The Shy Cog, the Stray Fanny, Dog's Leg, Lip and Jaw}

Is the line a *Fly?* Can it be released
And never further trap the rest?
                  Oh, there's two
    In a Twin-Cobblin', Kissin' Jennies, bes' t' part 'em…
Patient, working every hitch,
Breathing space between the threads,
Divining where a life has doubled back upon its past:
    Git it right at the last,
    And all will come un'notted of itself.

A' strings? A' strings?
Have you loom? Have you harp?
A' strings for me t'day?

Bleeding strings, throttled strings, crippled strings.
    They cut too quick, he says, beneath his breath:
    Impatient, wantin' free, leavin' ragged edges
    Left to bleed – worse, t' fray! T' ravel out,
    Vanish right away.

He searches under stairs and under beds,
Beneath the boards, and hid by attic dust,
Down between the pots of grains,
Or else entangled in the drains;
Perhaps it's in the cellar with the mulching pot,
Or caught within a tether in the milking shed;
Snagged upon a mattress spring, jarring in the harpsichord;
A sullen spinster's leavings, or a cat's plaything?
    If there's trouble, there's a 'notted string!

      {String, strand, line, thread, rope, wool, yarn, weave,
       Web, twist, cotton, peel, warp and woof, cable, fleece,
      Leather, net, chain and stitch, hemp, hair, sinew, vein.
      And gut.}

    Here's a 'not t' why yi' daughter flies int' yi' face,
    'N' why yi' wife is gripped in iron brow;
    T' why yi' son keels at the first, slights yi t' 'is 'orse;
    This 'not, I found within yi' drawer. I can untie it;
    First be warned that all that's bound within these loops
    And quand'ries will be freed around your 'ouse, yer ward,
    May even bring yi' market down!

I watched him work a gang of threads,
Caught behind a curtain on the bed,

Heard the lazy roof return to its place,
Saw the smile leave the housemaid's face,
Watched the mistress find her leg,
The husband learn to beg,
The son retread his flight,
The daughter disentangle from the night,
The baby find a song within his cry,
The aged grand-dame needing not a tear to glint her eye,
The river flooding gold across the floor,
The shaggy bearskin draped across the door,
And as he pulled the last neck from its noose,
I heard the words he said.

A' strings? Havya a' strings?

He'll ask you, Sir, to tie his boots, all buttons else:
I cannot tie – I mustn't tie – no loops for me! I only loose!

He'll loose the knot that draws the ship onto the rock,
That leaves the soldier rigid in the bullet's path,
The mother's hold upon the boldest son forlorn,
The sulking husband tugged toward the pretty eye,
Purse strings wrongly payed, too tight or over wide,
The swift chirurgeon's unhealed overstitch,
The mis-made and unfiring match:
So'times, a love 'not's t' draw apart, and then I weep,
Fer 'eartstrings shouldn't not be tied.
Is this yi' 'trothal rope, m'boy?
Aye, I c'n see she does not love;
I'll set yi' loose for a penny-ha'f –
He held the knot above the hanging cords,
Bristling knobs and loops, took a ragged end,
Drew it through a swollen hitch. The lover pitched,
Knees caught his flood of tears and knuckles
Kissed his forehead, tenderly.

D'na fret the lad, he said.

Easing with a rolling stroke, the bind surrendered
To his hand, trapped and choking lengths of thread
Unrooted from the tumbled scree.
The boy's convulsions settled, voicing free
His grief. He stood, at last, a crooked rope.
    Aye, kinks will stay a whil', but with hope,
    He'll tie it right agen.

He looked at me, the easy ties around my neck,
My cuff and calves, the high sides of my boots.
    Have yi strings about yi' persin?
    Makes yi strangle words tight upon yi' page?
    I can loose 'em so yi niver need t' bleed ink,
    Nor dip yi' pointed stick int' your soul…
I have no knots upon me, Sir, I say
With steady eye, nor tie. Just pen and ink.
    Aye, jus' keep yi' rhymes away –

    {Guilt, shame, secrets, ire, envy, loss, evil-grip,
    Illness, lies, fear, desire, lost belief, snarled lip,
    Cowardice, disdain, avarice, hunger, lust left and pain.}

A reader of birth-knots, life-knots, the slip-knot-death,
    (They say, the Elf will curse his name,
    Undoing quite their merry game)
He sees the weaving that the planets make, the stars:
    A holding 'not, a holy 'not, the warp 'n' weft!
    Ne'er t' be unknotted that –
    Fetters' work, the gods did that!
Drawing threads through heaven's loom –

That's good work, that,
Smooth work, niver 'notted –
Only so'times one goes back,
Missed a stitch – we feel it then!

But soon the 'Notsman finds the kink 'n' all is smooth once more.
All of us, patterns in a web, it seems, pulled – and pulling –
By more strings than may be known,
But get a 'not i' one, ni'one goes
Ni'where!

I must hide my 'scrawl' from the Knotsman's eye:
He'd take my tangled words, and smooth them out,
The knotted ink, to let my meaning fray.
Tied inside a *Double Cobbler,*
Hitched within a *Secret Shank,*
I keep my verse away from Knotsman's fingers,
And I pray, he will nev…

The Knotsman's Defence

Knots is good, aye. Knots
Is nay wicked. Knots
Is that which keeps yer sails
Strapped to the wind, yer bark
To the land, yer britches
Round yer bollicks, yer titties
Neath yer veil; what keeps
The fallen comrades knotted
Where they lay.
                    Knots
Is made the flight of birds
To summer and return, is fishes
In the sleepy rill and knotted sea;
Reefs and shanks and looping lines
Within the play of clouds
And turning stars. None
Would get much far without a knot.

But, when a promise doubles back,
Or in a yard, an inch or two
Is left to stray; or ay a ring is wrong,
And slipped onto the finger knuckle-ill;
A fight against the flood, or doors

Shut before the hinges will,
Then knots is made will snake
Around yer neck, will loop around
Yer cock and still his crow,
Will leave a hitch or two
Within yer mammy's pap,
And babies suckle-starve.
 Nought, but soundings muted, cleft and under-tuned,
 Will reach the strings within the infant ear.
 No one can be dear when
 The ill-made knot makes knots ill-made.

Then, 'tis time for picking, shaking
Dust from off the tangled thread,
Blowing space into the web,
Take the choking off a line,
And letting all hang free; feel
The rightness of the loom's warp,
The string within its proper key,
And, never snagged:

The bright and always telling yarn
 Thrum-m-m
Passing through the warp 'n' weft,
 Thrum-m-m
Humming tight and pulling true
 Thrum-m-m
Setting works aright and in their holy place.

In a knot, y'see, it will not work
To pull it tight, nor cut it out:
Cut it off, it's still a string,
But much too short to be a peace.
An' pull it tight, it does no more
But strangle on itself.

Take a look. Every knotted string
Is but itself
Drawn through a tunnel
Of its own loops and hitches;
To loose it is no more
Than but to push it back
Into a place it's been before;
To turn it bravely round –
        If I do it for a pound,
        I do it for a shilling!

So, turn again to face the place you've been,
And where it's tightest, where it's dark,
Walk through it once again.
Ye'll find it's but yerself,
With a kink thrown in!

Knot-Sure!

I sit in judgment of the shire,
As my father sat before,
In the place of God the father
And the founder of the law.
When all have seen the trial,
Heard the punishment in store,
I will string you in a minute
And tie the rope knot-sure!

The will of God is mine to speak,
Else why would I be here?
With wealth and lands at my command,
My justification's clear!
We need such disincentives
To hold in line the poor,
So I bind you to the gallows tree
And tie the rope knot-sure.

A mess of superstitions
Such as this I've never heard.
These yarns of yours, this picking
out of troubles is absurd!
The ways of heathen simpletons,
The learned must abhor!
So a scaffold for the lie you told,
And tie the rope knot-sure!

A cunning man? A juggler,
A mountebank, or worse,
A plying on the old-whim-wham
To prey upon the purse!
A string of gulls and ignorants
Is all you can conjure.
I'll have you dangle like a puppet,
Upon a rope knot-sure!

A single and almighty power
Has put you in my hands.
The only will of One above,
There are no other strands!
'Tis the devil you have knitted with,
Surrendered to his draw!
It will all prove your undoing
When we tie the rope knot-sure!

No ribbons on the water's shine,
No threads within the breeze,
No hitches in my daughter's lip,
No twist between her knees,
Nor no gripped up heart within
To make my mother me deplore!
More tight than ever she held me,
I'll tie that rope, knot-sure!

I dress my head with cap of black,
My hammer I bring down.
I sit the throne of mighty God,
And represent his crown.
I send you to his hanging tree
At edges of the moor,
And – quiet in the courtroom,
Such row must not endure!

Constable, your duty,
Make the prisoner secure!
This riot is against the realm,
And flinging that manure!
Captain, bring your cavalry
To scatter this furore,
Then drop them all from gallows high!
And tie the rope *knot-sure!*

The Slipped Knot

It frights me, this little learnin' I 'ave,
two letters to m'name – the c of the first curl,
and the s of the first shank, the pinch
to give the first three lines of m'trade.
Then most the rest is windin' and wrappin',
till ye've got two loops, one at each end,
then all's to know is where the neck goes.
The other gets the piglet, as you choose
one loop, pull it through to make a good noose.

It needs a strong beam too, a true tree,
plenty of room to let yer man dance free,
try'n' to catch the groun' with 'is feet –
'Ow many men wish they were taller then, ha!?
Pay me a shillin' and I'll dangle on his knees,
an' after, you might hear 'im, singin' low in the breeze.

I'm s'posed to hang aroun', haaaa! See 'im left
quiet on the 'enge, but a'times I pay a man,
enough rope, so t'speak, to keep an eye instead,
on the wide-brimmed one, the tree-rider,
come to question 'im, learn what he can.
I have no truck with such 'eathenry,
though I do let 'em touch me for the luck.

I only tie a knot, an' a slip-knot at that.
It's them as pulls it tight, with their weight,
pulling at the dirt when you'd think
they'd take the flight at any other turning!
So much fer too much learning, eh? Right,
it's time fer me to go. No! I did not tie it loose!

There was no room fer a goose to pull its scrawny neck through,
let alone a knotsman! Yes, he fell and he flew,
but if yer thinking of telling any other soul...

...I'll be dropping you.

'I'd ne'er deny the Knotsman, though he tied the rope hi'self'

The first knot I saw him loose was a love knot.
It were found upon the quay.
And as he teased the jenny from its crib,
They pulled her from the sea,
And, freeing the last loop from its den,
They breathed new life into her again.

It were formed of hair and hemp and the string of nets
Used by fishermen at their pots.
Water had got at it from the sea,
Left the tightest of knots,
But fingers nifty, fast and pointed at the tip,
Had brought her safe from sinking with the lost ship.

I saw him knock on a door red with plague,
No fearing, with the beak-faced doctors gone.
I did not want to go in, but waited
Through the night, pomander in hand, alone,
Sniffing, watched the candle in the night.
It'd made his fingers bleed, he'd said, it were that tight.

But in the morn, splinter-nailed, he came.
I had to catch him at the threshold,
While, laid within, breathing sweet,
The fevered kinfolk huddled from the cold
And threw their prayers at his feet,
And coin, for the laying out of yarns so neat.

I saw him draw the scar from off a man's eye;
Bring a soldier home, the last upon the field;
Loose a cargo from a rock; untie
A failing strand of barley, save a season's yield.
Walking away, with the livid strings dangled in his fist
Unknotted, like the smile of a lover kissed.

For me, he found me so ravelled I could barely talk.
He pulled me back a hitch,
Slipped a throttle, tugged it loose,
Showed to me the assassin's stitch,
And as he eased the bitter threads apart,
I fell into a fresh, believing heart.

So do not bid me curse the man who made
Me whole, or tell you where to seek;
If your own heartstrings cannot lead you to his pull,
In a day, or in a week,
Search yourself, search your attic, search your pots.
Or just listen for his cry...

'A'y knots?'

'My Mourning-knot is lost.' (or, The Knotsman's Farewell)

I found him by the oxbow, away from the new cut. He was looking through his case, his new case, for a picker he did not possess. He had a burn on his neck, but his eyes were knotted red.

> 'E were but a boy.
> They were b'th. But I loosed it
>   too soon. Too sharp and soon.

It was a knot in his own side.

> Should niver loose a 'not that is not ready.
> 'E felt it go, the boy. I know.
> 'E knew my ways, y'see.
> 'E'd seen me afore, seen me make a cloven-'itch
>   into a half-'itch
>   into a no hitch,
>   felt it for hi'self,
>   felt the freedom of a 'trothal-rope tied wrong, loosed.
> 'E had the touch,
>   had the nails,
>   scratched 'em down the other.
> He'd already fetched his sister to a better place.
> So 'e knew,

when I took the lines,
when I took the dog's end, when I first drew it out
from underneath the leg,
and 'e would know from the cold wind
blowing through the wynd
what I were to do.
The strings in the river pass too quick to be untied.
And the damn things bloat!

Agitated as a fray, he chomped against a halter. Never known a tether that could hold him. I have no art, and more despair than patience. I didn't know how to draw it out into a straight line. My own heart-strings, let alone his. Let alone, his always played a fair tune.

Take this.
Tie a knot around our fingers b'th. There.
Shall I draw my finger out, and so do you.
Pull it a touch.
Now keep it! Keep it safe.
'Tis a Mourning 'Not,
a Keen-'Not.
Keep it by yer 'eart, by yer soggy pap.
Keep it safe and when I'm gone, as I will, and as you're ready,
it'll draw the hurt, draw it like a diamond draws the light,
will shoot it away like a muskit.

Keep it till you're ready to unloose it,
Then take it out and tug
        on this one string 'ere, this red 'un.
Tug it 'ere,
        and all this long damn grief will be gone.

I put it 'ere, tuck it in,
Beneath yer smock, three ribs up.
So ye know where to find.

I saw him then take a rope, a simple rope of many threads, and short. It was unkinked, never tied, *only loose*, I heard him say. He took an end in each hand, crossed 'em over, wrapped one behind and passed it through the loop.

The elfs may have their vengeance on me now.

He pulled it tight.

Love Knot

See, beloved,
how I scratch my nail
on the side of your hand, push my knuck
in the deep of your palm, spread your fingers –
to kiss the smile inside, wrap my fist
around your thumb,
As I bend my brow
to press your cheek, clothe my ear
to meet your breath, as I lay my tongue
neat next to yours, set my hungry teeth
amongst your teeth,
As I step my sole
between your feet, as I wrap my knee
beneath your thigh, as I lay me soft
upon your hip, as I take you hard
in my hand,
As my belly pools
to the small of your back, as my rib slides
with yours into weave, as the hair of my limbs
takes root in your skin, as my blood enters yours
like a bruise,
As my mouth plays
psalms across the field, as I wet your pen
from my spit, as we glide across together
in a knot that never tightens, as I meet your face
lip to lip,
As I loop the swirls of my fingers
into yours, as I thread the spirit of my breath
into yours, as I tie the veins of my heart
into yours, as I bind the fate of my days –

31

APPRENTICESHIP

Knot

      Black thread comes in from the north,
    pulls a dog, passes through
  a barrel, then a hare, then another hare
 loops over twice, strangle grip,
falls away...
                  Green thread enters
           from the east, doubles back, sinks
              upon a kiss, rivers once on a hare,
                    rivers twice, tight on the teeth,
                            falls away...
           Red thread rears up
        from the south, hangs upon a jib,
      takes a dog, jaw then a leg, bitter
twist, river cog, falls away...
                       Blue
             thread claims to be a key,
              coming in from the west –

Knotlings: Children's Rimes

The Knotty-man, he comes and goes.
He'll loose your trousers and pick your nose.
Better to have no ties in your clothes.
No body knows what the Knotty-man knows.

Here's a knot!
What's it got?
Lips-drip and gubstitch,
Tickle-flick and grot!

Tie a knot about my finger.
Tie a ribbon in your hair.
Tie a knot around my winkle
When the 'notsman isn't there!

Half a hitch.
Half a hitch,
Puts the sheriff in a ditch
Let it fly,
Let it fly,
Sets the sheriff hanging high.

Elf upon my flaxen hair.
Elf upon my silver mare.
Tying tangles in the main,
Run when the knotter's come again.

Black crow, scare crow.
Laying troubles in a row.
Rook in an unhappy nest,
Black crow knows best!

Here's a string!
Here's a string!
Here's a rope,
And here's a king!
Here's a pretty neck-ring!

Thread 'n' flax 'n' yarn 'n' string,
Wicked girl entangle-ing

A shank to save a life
A cob to save a wife
No spit, no knife,
So the nutters say.

The Foundling

De ne touch the chil'.

Master, 'e will die.

Then let 'im die.

Ah woud tek 'im to the preost.

An mek a bindin' of 'im? We do not tie. We make ne bonds. Loosed 'e's been an loose 'e'll stay. Till the faer folk tac 'im mebbe.

Thar mebbe a mothir's lost 'im, or wud tac 'im fer a foundlin', sum unsucked mothir mournin' a bairn or wud tac on anovir.

'Is been lef, see, lef fer a changlin', lef fer the faer folk!

Ah'll find 'im a home!

Lef 'im be! Mus' I thrash 'ee? Stan thir, yong man, lemmee search thee out, thy pockets an' thy pouches! Ther's a knot upon ye, a bindin's been made abou' this loose scrag, an I'd unknit thee.

Ah will ne be parted. Thy fergiveness, I beg 'ee, but I wil nae put this chil' by...

Ye'll unpick 'is very death, will ye? Then ah release thee – ah cut thee off, a loose end, unmastered ye. Nay! De ne foller! Ah tac this swicce agen thee – swipe ye till the bark is stripped!

An 'e cut wide swathes upon me bac then, boy, wi' thee clutched in arms agen me gut and ches', an' who cried loudest of the three ah cannae guess. But ah learned sumwat from 'im that 'e cudnae teacce me, tha sum bindin's are not made but foun', tied by the stars mebbe, strong as sinew, not to be unboun'.

Ah foun' thee, la, wi'out a tie in the worl', an' me wi' jus' the one; me own master'd sought to cut our traces, but they 'ad already come undone; an' so we gan to gang together, we two, the unknotter an' 'is la'.

'The Route the Trouble Takes'

[Authenticity and provenance of this piece, with claims of an ancient
authorship, are doubtful.]

{*The Hare Loop, the River Loop, the Strangle-Grip,*
The Key Thread, the Loom Weight, the Fawn and Jib
The Shy Cog, the Stray Fanny, Dog's Leg, Lip and Jaw}

The loom weight is a weary pull,
a heaviness of head, hanging over shoulders,
gan back to bare a bristled throat.

The hare is a leap, long legs hanging,
arched over thistle; thrown to a dog,
it slips through spittle, sparks lightning.

The key thread claims the thoroughfare,
carried under canopy, cuts the hollow,
roots wreathed over; runs the gamut.

The river comes back, running to its mouth,
bites on its own tail, bright-teethed;
this loop learns what it longed for.

The cog is a heavy bird, catches in its bill
the boldest worms; binds the jenny
to the first light, flies in its shame.

Jib and fawn each have a jealous face,
squabble over the same eye; saying nothing,
the back of one is the other's bane.

    Dog keeps a lip lacing it with drool,
    shivers in the short, shaggy growl.

    Dog keeps a leg long kicking,
    long hours spent spearing air.

    Dogs keeps a jaw joyous over tongue,
    lunges in the wood with long howling.

The missing one makes all others:
tight around the heart, hurls a yarn
back upon itsen, braids notwithstanding.

The strangle-loop strains the stretched neck,
gullet in its grip, gorge must be hushed,
sat in the gap of a sullen gut.

The Slayed-Knot

Theyre iss no mendinge this, so stilly lie
Among the bracken broke upon the grind.
Yon thorn 'ut comes yer brething closely by,
A tyde of hurte as winces on ye wind,
Is bet to mind yee to a greater majestie.

In stilliness, the fellon acorne stands, its acre fill'd,
Yon apple swells to gladden up a mayden's choice,
An wool curls fram the lamb, the grain fram curage till'd,
That world of men allows itsen to hear a seconde voice.
The blud that runs the rownd fram heart and back is never will'd.

Such flaesh as fram these stillmost bones tends
Will have its thyme and then begone, and nothing mends.

The Spur

I follow him through threads of smoke, thick mud on our boots, and horses pleading. So many faces lying where they will, so many fires dancing. And is it a silence, or a din, this quell of battle?

He is so much bigger than me, my master, he has a sky about him. I marvel at his stride on most of days, and have to slip a hitch or two to keep his ways, but here, with such a mash, he's still as mountains.

Cum, la', he calls.

He dusna need the finer tools for what we're here to do. Jus' thicker boots. He steps into a pit of earth, a churn, and with his hooking hand takes up a wrist, a length of arm and lays it so. Then another's leg that overlies, and twisted too, he has to use b'th hands to shift it true. Another pair of limbs, a reset of a chin, an' then he's ready for me to help.

The fella lies beneath a cloak of blood. I would untie the cord, but me master flicks a neither with his eye. I'm to pull the shoulders while he watches for a snag or any dog-tooth tear. My first hoist just has me sliding. A better grip, a firmer foot, I feel him come my ways.

Above the pit, with me life-sweats gleaming, I'm told to drop him gentle, come around, and at his spurs I'm shown a knot all ruby-swollen, strings dripping wet. He knows me not t'cut, so steps away, leaving me with strings dripping like tears.

I'm picking at a mess of sinew, veins, not this our captain, but a nameless carl. Stepped in, he might have been. I lift each new *fly* from the sharp star, see it slip back into shape, see this trooper's leavings lie more easy.

Me master's with another, a man alive, speaks the charm, *Theyre iss no mendinge this, so stilly lie.* An' we wait, this unknown soldier's passing, his ragged breath to fray away. The knot of the fallen will keep them from rising, keep them comrades in th'eternal battle, in good if bloody company.

But our captain must be drawn away. Upon my back, he is a dead weight, but still I wonder is his wheezing real, or just the slam of his gut upon my bum. We get him to his father's tent, collect our fee. He has more colour beneath the beeswax candle. I look again at the cord around his neck. *We were n'paid f'that, la'.*

We washed ourselves above the weir, where no laundress could uz espy. But on the bank, before I dressed, he grabbed my gut. I've belly now, but then as smooth as glass, an' even so he found enough to hold.

This, la'. Dinna leave it so. Take it where y'must, but with your softly fingers, 'fore they get too hard, tease away the terror you have seen.

And then I screamed.

Then I wept, fiercely, thoroughly, angry at my knees, and keening through the fibres of my own blood, for every body butchered so and spilt across the country's floor. And every brother's son, or sister's heart.

It does not do to work a knot wi' anger. More as like y'll pull it further tight, but still, with someone's gut caught upon another's spur... *Theyre iss no mendinge this, so stilly lie?*

The Prize Picker (Or, a Knotsman's Recollections of the War.)

[Editor's note: This is believed to be a verbatim transcript, perhaps by the unknown scholar Mr. 'E.', although the parchment is rough and of poor quality, as is the ink, and the hand stressed. The words themselves have a dreamlike, visionary quality, or perhaps of delirium, or even drunkenness.]

Pulled oh as tight as a razor they were   *[The strings? Ed.]*
An' shrill to the fingers –
Not work to take em up and lose yer 'ands!
But the knot-thing they made needed to be something
An' they knew it!

How they zing'd, zing'd!
Like a new-made master's wall,
Or the leash upon a starvin' hound:
You couldn't see 'em for the sparks!
I lost me top third knuckle to it,
And the whorls on both t'umbs were shear'd
Like a lad's matted gone fer lice.
There were blood on stones that day,
And the two parties stood parti-colour'd afore me,
Ragged to the knees,
Bearded though they all were,

Even the maids,
An' bleary eyed,
An' clutch'd their loosen'd strings from the fray.

The nothing still roar'd,
One line reaching to the sky,
T'other bound to the machine,
T'other bound to the loom,
And each pull'd and pull'd and pull'd
As if it'd flip this tupside world aright again,
Though the king's neck had come unstrung
A long time ago.   *[Suggesting post-*
                                    execution? Ed.]

It were the only time I might have reach'd me knife,
Or took the captain's sword,
An' made a string to bleed.
But I took me prize picker with its pointy end,   *[Picker: a knots-*
Found the place it needed for to breathe,   *man's tool.]*
An' push'd it through,
Found the slip,
An' as I leant in to give it room to loose,
The thing pull'd tighter still!
Well! Me picker lost its pointy end,
But Heaven's string slipp'd its kink,
An' threw a loop out!

It was an easing of the ways that was –
I did not wake for a week!
And I dare say no king's purse would be rich enough,
 Nor no common wealth,   *[Related to historical events?*
To pay the pennies owed me for that prize picker,   *Uncertain, Ed.]*
Lost to the dog-star.

44

You'd wonder what it was could pull a string
To such a murderous tightness,
Tighter that a fat man on a noose, la' – *[la' – reminiscent of his master?*
But get them loose and thrumming like a zimmer-string… *Ed.]*
I could not see to see each end,
Nor step again toward them
For the shaking of the air,
Such a bite they had,
And me prize piker lying bent and sever'd,
White-hot forever more –
Like a ray of heaven coming through a cloud,
The only straight line in nature
You'll ever see,
An' the landward one like an archer's sinew
Keeping his fingers hook'd and his arrow cock'd –
That arrow's flying now and will ne'er be stopp'd –
But I'm whitterin' now,
Shiv'rin'. *[Is he in a fever? Ed.]*
Jus', right the strings, give em freedom…

And whichever team it is at either end
Can keep it tight as an horizon –
You could hear their dismal chatter on the line,
Like angry teeth clenching on a neck,
And feel it give.

Love-Not

I.
Look, can ye see?
This kink is th' first time she laid 'er bare feet upon 'is lap –
can ye fathom his surprise, la'?
And 'ere 'is 'eavy sighs firs' grappled by her arm,
ooh, she 'eld 'im tight!
An' these two threads 'ere,
see 'em walkin' in a twill
on a sunny afternoon;
such a thing will always lead to a bondin',
ye would think it would go well.
But 'ere's the secret twist
that gives a lie to so much promisin':
this Kissing Jenny is not a true tie at all…
Just a link 'ere at the bottom,
an' the rest just a jumble,
because this line 'ere is a mother's voice,
an' this white yarn is a father's shame,
an' all this long labyrinth of lives
gives it just the name of love.
But not a proper bond, no, not a proper bond,
I c'n loose it with one hand.

II.
Fond, no more than fond.
Yer command would 'ave me wrap it up
in a golden glistenin' thread,
But I cannot lie,
I cannot tie,
an' I cannot make a knot which is not!
I cannot make a little of a lot,
An' I cannot say I haven't what I've got.

I'd say, it's best to put a button on it!

The Black Thread

Ye must know of it, though I hope ye never meet it.
Should ye touch it, ye mus' needs mind the black thumbs it gives ye:
Gang greene isn't nothin', nor the bite of frost.

They say gold will mend, but those who have it
Will never know they've got it…

Ye'll see it in the eye of sailors pulled out of a sinking,
Though there be not much of them, who've seen the breach
and make it to solid ground…
… their mates and crewmen all gone down, la'.

Or of those who shine as bright as fire,
Into a flat and unwarming mirror.

And sumtimes in the newest mother,
Heavy in the brow as her belly's slack;
Niver mind how bonny the bairn…
It's a special kind of empty, that.

A clinging thorn aroun' the heart of one
Who cannot move as the earth does, an' so the world pulls away,
And there's the tear it spills from.

An' the killer's got it too, though he may 'ave murder'd not a one.

I think it a fear, and the fear of a fear,
Biting like a running seam, where every fresh stitch
Still pricks through, rancid, too tight on a fella's face,
Too dark in a woman's womb.

I know it is a thread of self-abhorrence, though unfairly sewn,
And it'll make a knotsman of anyone – Oh, untie it, man,
You'll hear 'em say! – but those to whom it's in the weave,
Ye'll see 'em take the pointed nail and tear not just the bind
But all the twists of all the spin,
As they could make it wool agen, put it back upon the lamb.

For all have known the break and felt the worthlessness slip in.
An' whatever knot you find it, there'll be no heart to it. No win.

Four Failures

1.   I've kept her swaddled longer. Father's not to know, he would not know, he would not know the creases in my face were deeper still, so short he is to look. He looked not once upon my face as we were making her, was pious in the chapel when she came, heard not a sound of my troubled labour then or now.

But he will ask and he will give me blame, as well he might, and even now I think to leave her by the open window, that the folk may take her back if they did bring her me. Or did they blight me so for some mistread upon their hidden roads? Oh, what's to do and what's I done to leave us crippled so?

I'll unwrap her. You need not touch her, or put a stain upon your own finger. Better it be me, who's 'ready blasted, than your blessed ways. Stay quiet, Bab, stay voiceless as I show this loosener your curse.

Oh, Master Knot! I pray thee, do not think me monster, mother of such a one! I say she's without legs, for whom would name as legs such skin and splinter? Who would call this child? Who would call this girl? Who would say that this was else but witch's spawn? I see the fire's lit for me! Else the hanging tree, that she, such a wasted thing, should be!

Can find it? Can you find the bind that keeps her knees a-twisted so, her thighs so chicken-necked, her toe so curled around? Can you stretch her ankles by a straightening of a thread? Search! Search the house, the birthing room, the chapel, chicken-run, what you will, and bring her loose and into walking 'fore her father finds the truth, turns me from his door, tells my mother what I failed to do, and tells her cruel she is not his and nothing of this earth!

2.   Sir, you know I am a pious man, a man of God, and know Him in my heart. And I have prayed for what He will not give. But love alone is moving me, greatest thing of all, to my own reading, and I know they say, in the village square and around their drink that you have ways to undo a kinked rope.

I have a daughter, sir, just come of age, and she is indeed the brightest thing upon the earth, the sweetest and most precious gift of many my beloved wife has given me. Since first I held her in my arms – you see I weep a little, holy tears, not a shame – I never was more moved, nor yet indeed before her birth, not even on my wedding day, nor any day in chapel, only one thing caused me pain. And that not for any flaw or imperfection in her frame…

But you will see, Sir, when I bring you to the garden where she sits, her happy brothers round about, her slight and air-blown body seems a thick and stalwart tree beside her legs, covered well for modesty. I forebear to let you look on them yourself, being not a gentle-born or studied doctor, but I will tell you that there is no flesh upon them, only slipping skin, nor no straightness either, and such a tightness in the string inside, the withered sinew, that they must draw up like a sparrow leg, and could not bear even such a weight as one.

Thank you for your napkin. No, I have my own. Sissy, please, a handkerchief! I shall keep my tears at bay, if I might. The wars, Sir, have not been kind to me, my fortune has been lessened and my faith, and my health is shortened too. I fear, unless her legs be mended, for her life, once mine is done. So I pray, firstly that your ways be no 'ticing of the devil, though my soul I'd rather peril than her happiness, and that you work your art, your loosing art, upon the knotting of her joint and sinew. Please, begin.

3.   She is my life and so I beg you, free her from this evil grip upon her knee and thigh. I will pay you both, your man and you, in silver or in gold. Please, sir, your younger eyes must guide him on his way.

Ah! I see, those old and pinching fingers are wise, with agility my scribing hands would lack! Yes, sir. Let us leave him to his art. We can bring a candle to him, no? Has he got such feeling skill, even in the dark? Then my hopes are raised again. Yes, let us tap some spirit, to ease our night, as he does his work...

The house is quiet now, the boys asleep, her fine and infant brothers. They have come to us, her parents dead, and they become the children we will never have, and she will need legs then! So, I am told! I never asked that of her, nor for her, not till now, not upon our wedding, nor even when we met upon the Summer's dance, and I could only lift her in my arms and swing her round within the fiddler's play, and throw her up beside the drum, and grip her lightly-tightly as the whistler on his pipe. I carried her in courting, and I carried her to wife, across this threshold here, I...

Perhaps, upon the morrow, when she wakes, she will find beams hanging from her hips, or like the sarsens holding up the hanging stones! Is he done? These the strings? Then thank you, Sir, your silver! No? Pennies then, if that's your wish, and a shilling to your man for the use of his ears! Ha!

Goodnight, gentle... Um, goodnight. Yes, I retire now, join her in her sleep.

4.   I have had a full and happy life, in spite of what was promised. For all I have not stepped one foot upon the earth, I have danced, married well, brought my mother's boys to manhood, been a mother of mine own, boy and girl. You may have heard, sir, I am a cripple since birth – my legs all left behind in my mother's womb, perhaps, and skinnier than bone is what was left me. And such a tightness in my sinew, tis a miracle I ever could conceive, carry, bring to term, and teach them both to walk! I cannot tell the fear and joy to look upon them both, with legs as strong as oak, and as straight as ash, when the earth-wife brought them to my breast!

And my husband so in glee and so full of loving me. I would call him a looser of knots also, for the freeing work he did upon my heart and soul. That I should outlive him…

Now, there is nothing more beneath Heaven I would ask but only this, and I hope your fingers' skill and ancient art may serve me so. And though your master is no more, just as mine has gone, and we must each work alone, I bid you search. Search the house, search the garden, search the pantry and the loom. Find the knot that binds me! I would walk, sir! Walk, if it be even a faltering step. Ever did he carry me, and now he cannot, and I would walk my husband's coffin to his tomb.

His Master Freed

I would unravel the ground if I could,
    flick aside the threads of earth
    in clean string –
but I must dig, scraping up
    the loose dirt
from the shallow hole it overfills.

No moon to show my fingers,
    only touch, but soon
I feel the ridges of your face,
    puffed and soft, and cold
    like a mountain mere.
I feel the hair of your brow
    unknotted, and the stubble
    sprouted on your dead cheek.
I clear your mouth of clods,
    find your throat, find the rope.

It's swollen as your neck is swollen.
    Makes it tight, makes it cling
    against itself, with no more slip.
They've given you the whole length,
    thrown into the pit, and must pay
    the pennies to hang another.

The henge above us stands stripped.
But I must work my strongest bones,
my fiercest grip, to waive these wet lines,
    well fed wyrms,
      from the loop,
         the loop,
         the loop,
         the loop,
         the noose!

Hoooose!
The air goes home!
The head falls back,
the jaw's ope!

My master!

I felt him settle then,
felt him lie with a soft laaa'…

I owe tha' Mother Lichgate ha'f a shillin'

I bring ye this, Knotsman!
Mother Lichgate says she saw me
wand'rin' in the bury-yard the late
on Midsummer's eve! Says
she sits there ev'ry year,
says the church-porch is her place
to watch the apparitions
walking to the portions
will be theirs. Says she
saw my face, an' that a white-un,
ferrying my ways, an robb'd
of all my wares, an' not
a penny in my purse! Unknot
this, man! An' save me life
for another year. My wife-was
waits fer me in a dank grave.

> *Thy thread is what it is,*
> *Ah cannae mak it longer,*
> *buh this at least,*
> *when ye do go, it will*
> *not be to a wander,*
> *but to a lie in peace.*

LOOSE THREADS

The First Knotsman?

Thy mothir's taecn fer a wicce
N trussd inter the borogh gaol,
N thee mus hide thy hid as well
Else snaggéd be by follow-sticce.

He took hissen to hollow hill,
His granddam's secret bury-place,
N there he hid his sorryd face
N tore his tatty shirt, until

A kindly hand of knotted lace
Was felt upon his sholder drawn,
Mor soft'n light of summer morn,
him minded to his mothir's race.

He taec the scatterd ribbons torn,
N hied him to the miller's pool
N saw em set the ducking stool
Upon the green n sodden lawn.

The night he spent in shaders cool,
A-connin all the bindin ropes,
The shanks n hicces, strangld loops,
N heard agen his grannie's rule

Of like-fer-like, so boundn hopes
Began to loosen: when his mam
Was dunken under, off she swam!
But taen agen, in metal hoops

They bound her tightly, brought her home.
Her proven guilt mus judgment have:
The magistrate, her sowl to save,
Said she mus ride to Neckingham!

Scratchin at a hangd-un's grave,
Beneath the crossd-road's earthy grip,
He took the swolld n cnotted-slip
That ghast had from the body clave.

With grannie's words upon his lip
He worked the coild murder loose
N saw the execushner's noose
Offer up no fellership.

The magistrate had nought to choose
But bear her straight into the fire,
N that became her funeral pyre.
Tugs n pickers had no use,

The threads of flame aweavin higher.
Fore the blaze was dampen down,
His wide-brim hat upon his crown
He went, a wanderin untier,

He roamd the countryside aroun.
Loosin all the troubld ropes,
N cnotted cares, a-kindlin hopes,
Is how thy cnotsman came ter town.

The Undoer of Knots

The priest is loosing knots within the church on Sunday morn,
Says loosing is the Saviour's work, the reason He was born,
Reciting all the miracles He'd done through His sojourn,
And we all would be free on His returning!

He didn't like the Crow they call the Knotsman coming by
To the houses of the parish, with that cunning in his eye,
Saying, Give me up yer strings and I'll unknot them by and by,
Tis not a mickle fee I'd be earning.

Him's unhappy of a magic that was older than his own,
So he's got his bishop's blessing, and his candle, bell and gown,
And he's got a mat of tatters, with the ribbons hanging down,
In the pulpit, full of glee at his learning.

And he's plucking at a Jibber, and he's pulling off a Fly,
And he's thumbing at a Fanny, with a twinkle in his eye
And he's whipping out the tangles of the trouble merrilye,
Full of all his scholarly discerning!

The squire and his family were sitting in their pews,
The congregation all around to listen to the news;
Well, he wasn't very happy when the squire lost his trews,
Had 'em falling to his knees on his turning.

And his mistress had a shock when all her corsellage it burst,
Had her flopping on an altar boy; that must have been a first,
Had 'em leaping for the vestry, and in their hands they pursed
Such fine and rosy cheeks, red and burning!

And the village all in hooples, with their marriage bonds awry,
Turned to kissing all and sundry, throwing britches to the sky;
Such a casting off of petticoats, you had to turn an eye!
The wooden man green in his gurning!

And the priest cried out, My Saviour, why have you forsaken me?
Your grip upon my hand is gone, and I am fallen free
And alone as any lost and common thief upon the tree,
Never to be released from this yearning!

Well, the village settled down again upon a summer's day,
The priest he found his mission in an abbey far away,
And the Knotsman saw the mat of tattered ribbons where they lay
Sang, Ay' strings for me?

The Chirurgeons

He described the hurt in layeman's terms,
As being to the left of the breast bone,
Fourth rib from the collar,
Just where they meete, and at a depth
Indeterminate, but less than the heart.

There was no mark upon the skin, nor scar,
That could be seen by candlelight or sunne,
To front or back. Tho pressing on the spot
Induced a fit of tears and a down pull
On the corners of his mouth, and a wail.

By his report, he fancied it a pinch
Or twist within, or mayhap like a stone,
An arrow head, or else a lead pellet,
Though, curious, not fired from a gun,
But dropp'd through the water of a shot barrel.

A tender pin prick, he called it. A knot
Of feeling pull'd deep and tight. A clot.

> Our study and discussion could discern
> No likelihood of mortality from 'the wound',
> But the man would often fall to weeping, clawing
> At the fabric of his smock, to be free of it,
> And evinced such distress, we did pity him.

And offer'd to induce in him a heavy slumber,
Promising him release from pain and sought
Beneath such sleep to probe what lay within.
For sure, we must excise the bone and risk
His blood and air to enervation. But,

If we might discover this sharp diamond,
Cut it free, and leave the soft flesh unmolested,
Who would not consider it a mercye?

The poor wretch died upon the table,
Beneath the knife, fighting with delirium,
And spitting froth. We took our leisure then,
In peeling back the skin, unhooking each
The muscles of his chest. Alas, we found

No diamond, nor indeed any knot or stone,
No shot twisted beneath a short fathom,
But only, now unfeeling, meate and marrow.

The Poor Knot Amongst the Rich

I laid my body out the length of the vine,
hitched the scion to the rootstock, teased
the arms, tied knots into a bunch beneath,
squeezed them into loose and running wine.

I laid my body out on a front line,
swinging out the heavy blade, shield
lodged above my brother, muscles sealed
into knots, bodies laid out, knotted, dying.

I knotted barley into stooks upon the field
as my wife plaited dough into bread,
had all our little hitches at the table fed,
from tying seeds to the furrow, a harvest yield.

I took the strings of thought within their head,
reefed one upon another, made a net
of knowledge, learning never to forget,
set them turning, each with their own new spun thread.

I laid my language into verse, set
my words about a scream refined,
the knotted tortures of my mind,
reminders of my lover's debt.

The many threads of lovers' kin we combined
in a finely bound betrothal rope,
celebrating union and future hope,
laying both our bodies intertwined.

I laid my body out when the waters ope,
pouring into ribbons on the bed, on her thigh,
knots tied into the cord, the bleeding knife by,
born beneath the strings of a fresh horoscope.

I laid my body out across the breast of the sky,
stars feeding out of the milky way, looming
light and patterns into this worried glooming,
such knots as planets make through eternity.

The Hill-Diggers

The strings are bleeding, the strings
are bleeding out!
The hill-diggers, blasted in their fear,
fell into rout,
and the knife would take each one of them in turn
from ear to ear.

It was amongst the Easter Barrows,
midnight moon,
by blade-point and cutlass,
the cunning-men taken down
to find ancient gold
for the hill-diggers' purse.

The diviner with his 'Moses Staves'
had bid them ope
the Sleeping-King's Brow,
fed their hope
with a keen assertion,
but finding now

nor any silver, but the moon's,
nor any gold,
save ruddy earth, with shovel's haft,
diggers 'gan to scold
the geomancer's feeble limbs, only stopped
when the Knotsman laughed

and told them tales of dragon spirits
lurking on the hoard,
would blind their eyes to treasure's show,
But 'ear me word,
there is a way t' loose the serpent's bind,
'nd this I know.

Search aroun' the 'ill, or on yer cart
or in yer coat,
and if ye fin' a knot entanglin'
a matty rope,
bring it us, an' fin' a way we shall
ti 'ave it danglin',

an' tha' will loose the stubbornest of wyrms.
For most of night
they cast about and found at last
a knot that might
present the dragon's bond, a sodden rope
bound thick and fast;

they brought it to the Crow. *I tell thee now,*
there's nought t' do,
but me to 'old the Trouble, an' thee
ter cut it through,
an' tha' will loose the dragon's bond,
'nd set it free.

Moon sharp, the blade point was entered,
pushed into the work,
and as the edge sliced through the thread,
a sudden lurch
jolted both the digger and the crow. All stared
at strings running red:

The strings are bleeding! The strings
are bleeding out.
The digger's gang whipped themselves into fear,
running with doubt
for their safety, ran for their lives, left
the Digger-King standing there,

holding tattered strings in his hand,
staring at the tear
in his wrist, threads of blood spooling out,
at the glare
in the Knotsman's eye, cruel gleam
in the red pooling.

Ne'er ti cut, my man, it is no use
ti bring a blade
ti what must with patience be unpick'd
an' careful laid.
Wi' ye own malice, murd'rin' greed,
yer own life's prick'd.

JOURNEYMAN

The Bag of Ribbons

'Tis a very thing of beauty that, yer little pouch,
And fill'd with all variety of twill and snatch
Of cloth, so many remnants left to pore upon.
You'd 'ave me give 'em quite a turn.

Open it, she said, me little bag is knotted up some
An't needs a finger's work.

I've niver seen such a pretty knot of fur 'n' fibre in all me
            knotted days,
So easy 'round me knuckle. If I stir it with me 'and,
It gives a sweet aroma, like yi've kept and instillated
Every kinder perfume in the weave.

Draw it out, she said, this ribbon's pink and threaded through
With glistening silver too.

I hope I've not a nail to catch yer, can't be doing causing yer to fray,
Or loose yer precious swatches. This twist around mi pinky,
Is not that the softest cloth ye'll ever feel? Oh,
Ye are the fairest weaver of the finest skill!

Breathe it in, she said, I'd have you take it to the deepest,
All the heady scents of my life's best.

It were a simple bag of ribbons, kept in velvet pouch,
And every one, she said, the memory of a time.
And looking at them each upon her lap we went
Beyond her eye, and under mine. Such magick.

I am wove, she said, and I have woven.
I thank'ee, knotsman. And then she kissed me, went her way.

The Weaver Wife

Would 'ave me bind ye in a knot?
I cannot tie! I cannot twist
The strings of a nover's 'art…

This is what he said to me. This
He took for why, and never looked
If we might lie as woven threads and kiss,

But side by side, and never kink or crook.
A weaver I, beating fibres
With a sword into their proper nook,

I laid a loom about him – gentle jibes,
He would not lie within my arms
For more an hour's pass, the feared'st of all his tribe.

A proud man then, I let my fleecy charms
Raise him high, and how his shuttle flew
Between my warp and weft, in spite of his alarms!

He did not know what strings he threw
Beneath my thigh, nor what a knot
Began to tangle, nor how it grew…

Because a bonded looser I had got!
And never mind the ways I tried to hold him,
He was gone before the first clot,

Before my mother had the chance to scold him!
The baby does not cry. It sleeps,
Though with a bundled brow, as I enfold him,

And just the memory of his father seeps
Beneath my thigh. My husband starts
Beside his pretty weaver girl and in his slumber weeps.

So did he bind me in a knot?
Well, not so tight to leave me mourning what I've got.

Midwinter

I.

Oh my, but this mass is a time of knotting en't it?
Wi' the carols and the very many songs
threading through the hall, an' the yarns
spun out as Winter-tales, to waste the longest night,

wreaths hung all about of Holly, bay
and Rosemary, these the maids cam
with cakes, with wassell cakes and jolly wassell,
white loaf and cheese, minst pyes

and meat, the jolly youths and plaine-
dealing Plow swaines fell to dancin',
to show 'em Gambols and breaking of shins,
an' then the kissin' bush gets a crowdin',

while those as don't or won't or will not
be kissed c'n chance a scalding of their lippes
to bite the apple, else the candle,
wi' the log lit from the last year's yule...

an' they seek to cut it off like a king's neck?
Here cam the small ale fer all the bairns...

II.

I shall leave it untouched for now, for this
is a midwinter month and i have no fingers.
i shall leave it bruised, a knot of blood, a flood
through still water. The serries will remain,
ridges on the roof of a mouth, and i
shall leave the smoothest parts untongued.

A heart sometimes can only take
so much blood; lungs only so much air.
A BELLY HAS MORE GIVE. These hands
can only hold. A mind,
deep or shallow, needs wallow.

A bleak light through the window breaks;
a slight thaw makes the water drip,
the silence bloats like a drowned corpse
risen, and stillness doesn't go anywhere.

An' when I do return in a grown month,
in a year-ha'f,
Ye shall see a May-tide blaze in the field.

The Scholar in his Cups

Knotsman, tell me,
is not each tongue itself a string of knots?
Each word a bound mass of meaning?

In speaking, it is so easily forgot
what ties lie in another's ear,
so what we say is rarely what

they hear…
As if the threads of our many learnings,
taught by hope, by fear,

caught up in, oh, so many yearnings,
should, so tightly bound,
send these 'loose women' to their many burnings,

throwing sound
unravelled, onto pyre,
or silenced under water, drowned.

'Evil', 'ill' – what a knot is there: a 'Sire
of the Damned', calling
each to eternal fire?

or a simple work of elements, appalling
and inimical to health and well-
being? Such an angel falling,

or the clear wisdoms that foretell
how an imbalance of humours
will lead to bile, phlegm, the swell

of tumours,
and evil death? This science,
against superstitious rumours

of evil-eye,
and curse,
must cut away, violently,

those black and worser
threads. And 'Love',
– so often bound in verse,

another faggot shoved
upon the blaze –
is not that word above

all others for its maze
of convoluted
meanings? Threads in a haze

of fog, fluted
aspirations and conspiracies,
in secret chambers mooted

and then abandoned; rhapsodies
of godly fervour
and sacrifice; remedies

promised by a favoured
eye, or breast;
succour from a missed mother;

promises from the priest;
the dull, thudding
thrust of a beast's

rutting...
tell me, Crow!
if the gutting

of these heavy words, thrown
so lightly,
with all extraneous meanings thus disowned...

will it not somehow, leave us more free?
Or will you persist, black-feathered stump that you are,
in sitting silently?

Scrawl, or Calling on Mr E.

I saw a knot upon a poet's lap,
a tangl'd ball it were,
of wire, gut, of hair, an' twisted strand.
I rose to tap it loose,
but 'e moved into study,
shut the door,
started throwing 'is words around,
wi' cries of soft despair and weepin',
rage and wild pain.
When 'e open'd,
I foun' the knot was gone,
but ink'd ont-to the page
was such a mess of writin'.
'E was calm,
while the wordage fired,
as who would choose surrender to the gallows-cart:
'arm done, time to don the 'angman's slippy noose.
I felt I saw him snare 'i'self upon a poacher's nail,
        when I could've undone.

The Poetess

Sit thee down now, Miss,
'n' don once more yer shift.
I swear, I did not ask ye to be stripp'd,
nor bear so rare a stripe.
Here's a napkin fer yer eyen.

I foun' no knot upon ye,
nor yer room, though plenty
'round the 'ouse – thy Da's
a proper-mither'd cock, 'n' the mouse
that nips yer mothir makes a right mock!

Ha! I've got ye smilin' now!

I have no bindin' fer to loose
ye from, but only this…
Can yer tell me what it is,
swirled all about like threads of blood
upon the water, washed against the mud?

Black spider threads scratched upon a page:
I see they find reflection in yer face.
I'd 'ave ye speak 'em, but I fear them.
These lines, I cannot unbind 'em, not 'ere,
much less once they're join'd to the air.

An' now ye weep agen. I'm sore fer that.

Thy kin've no patience fer yer pain;
they'd call it shame. An' I c'not unstitch
the words you've risted here in rhyme.
That's the world's now,
'N' ye must learn to live in it any how

ye can.

The Sailor

He would not touch it, this one,
Though he saw me so
Bound.
He took my hand, opened it, planted this
Gang
Of yarn, cords and fibres,
Closed it again, into a fist.
I can't go
Home,
I said.

He said, *It is a hard thing to be a Da',*
I know,
So far from 'em and not in their days.
but there's babbys' hair in that,
an' I will not loose it.
Yer wudna thank me fer it if ah did.
Just as
She
carries scars within the womb, they within her arm,
carries they into 'em's life, so
You
will carry too. In your side. N'matter how
Distant.
Ah shan't leave ye
To bleed,
like a feeding cord no one thought to see,
an' none a ken it
Needed to be tied.

I have a hank of strings, I have,
Formed in a far country, across the seas.
And here upon a rolling deck, men around,
Knowing sorrow, none there is to blame me,
But a bonny boy and girl.

The Puritan

A man of great age.
With so many strings upon his face.
Paper skin.
Ancient skill in his fingers still.
Breath is an old friend,
and his thought has learnt to wait.

He has never sat here before,
his back not bowed so
for fifty years or more.
The noise keeps to the other side of the room.
Just him and the Crow,
in their own cellared vintage of shadow.

A mix of strands and fibres,
almost as light as the bones in his hand,
laid in his palm. (A saviour's wound,
or devil's mark?) Held
by a simple reef, perhaps
the last knot of his life.

'This old idolatry remains.'
He says, 'These fetters.
'These knots and shadows of ill-made fortune.'
I cannot unbind this,
but by my hand. No prayer, no faith,
to loose it, but to discard it

still tied...'
But he let the Crow take it,
watched the clawed fingers tap the tightness
from the knot, give it back.
He himself pulled the last head
from the noose.

'I think I feel forgiveness,
Knotsman. Who can tell,
But I? And this knot untied.
No impulsion now. Landlord!
A luncheon for this man!
I must spend my last shillings well.'

Blood-Knot
(or, The Weaver's Child)

'Don't ye dare to take yer fingers to these strands! I swear ye'd loose the sinews round yer ragged knees, the blistered veins upon yer cheek!'

The threatened smack hovered falcon over, but did not come down. Instead, she gripped him a talon gaze and watched his pads number out the braided threads. With him quiet, she could land gentle on his neck.

'The blue one look, the soft azure, that's yer father's mother's line. That's where ye get yer grace, yer hooking smile. A sinless one her, that for all the pulpit says. I'd fall in love with her meself.

'The red one, bold, that's yer father's vein, his father's too. See how it looks as links within a chain, that's to show the life must jump a gap, but in a mother's mother's, see it spills and spools as solid as a hair.

'But to yer fathers' – that's a bloody-minded streak, the one that fights the wars when there's no skirmish to be done. Gobby too, hush yer! I knows. And all from a nobleness you'd squirrel away.

'Mother's father, that's a dogtooth, jagged as a knife, mine is too. Never, for an age, did a mother's father's line run smooth, except among the happy ones. He disappeared, ye know, she held him up so high. In there's yer wandering, there's yer disappearing in the dell, but then calling in the market, wi' yer a' strings! But 'tis a line that wanted to snap straight, though the warp would never let it.

'And this, yer mother's mother, and her mother's mother too, that's the breath within yer lungs, the flesh within yer saggy skin, all the weight that keeps yer line tight. Ye'd no more loose that than the kiss ye left upon me lip upon a lost summer, the pinch that stings still upon me pap and puss.

'She's a rainbow thread indeed, of all the lights – ye did not know, I trow, what's woven in a sun's beam – but there's the fitness in you to feel the thread and give it free, because ye know in yer thrumming heart what is choked and what spurts happily.

'And if you 'ravel it further – hush, now! Still yer picker! I speak but in magery, not in doing, nor in undoing ...less those yer britches grow too tight again as once they did before... give over with yer age! – if ye 'ravel it further...

'What a braiding here. There's warping here that shows yer father's mother's da, and all the delving deep they did in word and rock. Proper copper, they. And here's a mother's father's father, foster child spliced into a kin from 'cross the sea – brought a weaver's magic same as me.

A father's father's mother, bore an empty man's name to keep her from a beggar's shame, though she loved 'im much who give it 'er. An one more I'll read ye fore we lose the number of 'em, here, yer mother's mother's father, what a flame here, hungry for the knowing of the master's lore.'

She watched him stroke the braid a while with his fingers, eyes and air, the knots that need no loosing, the strings that lie together, gently cross in such a tender warp 'n' weft.

'Will ye look at this one now my sweet, before me husband flounders in again and spills his rye and barley on the floor. See it's all the lines of your own threads and here's the lines of mine. Can you see how, in this merry jigging of the pattern how the two combine?...'

He did not heed her further words, but left them to unravel. So did I. For then he looked up his crooked hat at me and met my eye.

MASTER

Knot Love

I went to the knotty-man. He
was sat in the market, knees out,
stopped his talk to the gentle,
beckoned me to.
                    My fingers bent
so keen upon it, he had to open
them first to get the rope. But
then he looked and when he spoke,
she does not love,
                    I broke, I
floundered like a ship bestormed,
I wept then, and as he wormed
the lines from the loops our fathers
made, I held to my knees,
                    carved
by his tenderness, knew that
the string would not be straightened,
only hang free, that the kink
it betrayed was something
    I could never
                    put to ink...
That I do not love... her, beloved,
That I could not love... her, beloved,
That I could knot, so moved... beloved.
Your shamed eye cast down, your hair
afire, I raise your hand to this prayer
    See, beloved..

The Knotsman at Rest

He sleeps with his feet to the wall.
All the threads of his face fall away,
as linen settled over one sent to peace.

Breath passing like bliss through a loom –
I ran my hand across it: the raising of his breast,
the hollow of his stomach, lightly fleeced…

So many freed! He practices what he preaches,
loose limbed, hanging soft – what a banging it would be
if I touched him now, such a gentle drum.

It is a hard thing, best passed kindly over, the tug
of warmth, blood beneath another's skin, calling like a sun,
and the want to bind, to steal the last stook from the field;

a hard thing to leave the edge unhemmed, to fray –

> I'd tease out his hair should he leave off his hat:
> I saw an elf guarding it, spear-grass ready,
> while his lily-white lover played out her spite.

– but I would not risk waking him into such a day.

Oxbow

All so much is felt as all unstrung these days; an empty frame, me, with nowt to 'arp upon. An' 'ow c'n ah sleep neither, when the bind jus' sprang apart in me 'an's.

I dun't know what it were that brought me 'ere, the floody river by, nor to this hangin' strand. Ah could watch the silver lines upon the water-top an' all the words they made; an' if ah cud remember, ah think they'd say, come. come with us this way.

I drifted onto 'em, drifted up as they were. No steps upon the sand, but mine. They'd not walked it, nor swam. They were still as swans, with my heart kicking. An' lip to lip, all bound they lay.

The sheets were from off their bed an' wrapp'd about they wrist, and held them each both once and holy, tum to tum, an' arms around, a swollen, soddy mess, all soft 'n' drown'd, 'n' like the river, ah did not know to weep or rage.

But I look'd upon the knot 'e tied and read the meanin'.

> *To the knotty-man: Sir, I bid thee read these knots before you loose them. You saved my life ere now, your kind 'clen' fingers working. Stay a while and do not let them cut – niver t'cut, you said. I have a penny-ha'f for thy trouble.*

> *My love, it is an arrow sent. The straightest line in nature. Where it went is not to be retraced. Neat, the path it made still lies in the air, sweet poetry, and found a chord in answer, thrumm, thrummm, I grasped it like a thumb within my fist.*

Though I might have been a knotsman bound, your keen apprentice, born of kinks and twills, here was something never to be pulled apart. The cords of the knot of a human heart, even tugged to loosen, cannot bear the cold of separation once they're tied. Like a coming out of bed, on a winter's morn, before the fire's lit. Such distance? Well, the water seems a warmer place beside it.

Tell my sister not to grieve for me. There is space between the weave to be free.

Ah waited till they found us, did not touch the bind, but let them pull it loose. I took the penny, laid it on his tongue, put the ha'penny upon the other one. With a ha'pence of my own, two ha'fs to make a whole.

The Betrothal Rope

I think Miss J has never been sure of owt, but her brother's love. To see her sweetheart William rigged in all his model gear, so dark and hard in helmet and plate, it made her doubt the more. Soldiers of every stripe were wont to play pike, as they say. But he had not thought to see battle so early, nor with one so slight.

I'm laughing now, but as the dawn broke I were as fearful as a fever. And she was raving, screaming round the house, calling for her betrothal rope and how it could not be found.

'It's undone', she'd shout. 'It's been slipped, and he'll betray me with a red-head wild-girl.' And oh, a water-jug lost its usefulness then upon the stone grate.

Well, I thought I'd calm her with the finding of it, wrapped inside her pillowcase, intact, of course, with his fingers still on it. She's a one to make a weapon of anything – well, she's lost so much – I just missed reliving my years with the tanner's wife! I'd forgot I could be so nimble.

When we heard his hooves in the courtyard, the thunder moved out of doors. The horse proved its nerve then, though stable-Tom let go its halter. She broke all over her sweet William, and though he has a tongue or two, his word were powder left in rain to her lashing and crying.

I could barely hear him make his protest, troth intended, sure to return, and she his Missus truly tied. When she said she would break it, lightning would not more clearly show the stark of his face. And though I never saw him fight harder for her love or life, slender though she is, so was his captain's sword and she was sharper.

But I did not know true fear till I saw the black crow by the gate amongst the village crowd. A good many had gathered round to see her flare, but he was sat unheeding. Still, the shadow of knot-dust and feathers marked him clearly out. When Miss J spied him – I saw her stop, I heard her thought – every fibre of me fell like a dropped spool.

The 'trothal rope was in her hand, its mark on William's face, and though it held still, I knew that here was one before whom nothing held its binding. Like spindle pulling thread she strode her way through the unravelled crowd, William unseamed behind her, the blackness in her heart darker than all the child-fears she'd hid from all but me, and she threw that lover's rope right into the Knotsman's lap.

Was she expecting it to burn like fuse, or fly away? I think meself I thought to see it unslip in his hand, or snake away like a gang of worms, the morning bird disturbed. William was a face distraught, to see his precious heart-strings thrown to the raven. The crowd was clutched. Miss J stood like one on the verge of freedom from fear and feeling.

He looked at it, the Knotsman, fallen on his black breeches. He stayed still and silent. Then he took it up so lightly in his white-sinewed fingers, pointy-nailed. It seemed a captive bird in his hand, a gleaming jenny-wren, so like to fly, but strangely too at peace. She might have been in her own nest, with all her fledglings roundly fed. And perched upon that rope, all the knots and twists they'd tied upon it, Willy and Miss J, seemed just as happy. And every single one of them held.

I saw him then place that betrothal rope back into her hands. She was stiff now with fears turned from losing William's love to losing William's life. The Knotsman drew a finger down her brow. I was aholding her shoulder by now and heard his 'Din't mither.'

William was stiff too, beside us, head drawn back. His father's church and teaching was bleaker than ours, but he suffered the Knotsman to unbind a twist or two of his over-tight chinstrap, straighten a string at his neck. 'That'll bring ye safe back agen, la',' he said, 'An'll see ye do no great harm in Irelan', tho' there's many as will.'

Then he turned, walked away, leaving only his musty smell.

Turning

It   is   nae   a   knot.   Nae   a   knot.   it   can   be
loosed no further. It is not to be unpicked. It is not to   be
unspun. It is the unbindable thing. It goes deeper   than
a kink. It goes further into twist, into the yarn,   to the
string, a smooth sided stretching, spinn-   ing, furth-
er back, along, to beyond the other   end, and to
the new, to the turn, to the real   beginning, Now,
it goes to the spinning, Now,   they're spinning
it Now, fibres carded into   rolls, pinched, drop-
ped, spun, within a   moment, in this moment,
Now, little hooks   latching onto little tendrils
too small to   see, Now, all the wisps grow-
ing into   whispers, pulling from the cloud,
gath ered on the distaff, the next leng- th
of line, the wool growing loudly   on the
sheep's back, hand-plucked   from the
fleece, all the wool   pulled into a
single thread   of moments in a
life spin- ningbindingfibresof
the wooltwistingoutofnothing
intothreadstringlineyarn rope
nowintointointo   notaknot
thatevercanbe untied-onlycut

Ne'er t' cut, la'. Nay, niver t' cut.

Samaritan

I never saw a more naked man.
Loosed, he ran in thin runnels,
  threading through streets,
  as he might have freed himself from skin.
I saw strings hanging, untied,
  from the stars, around him,
  an unpulled marionette.
If the moon had a hand, it would come up empty.
The earth's palm, if it were, would close on sand.

All bond to mother, master, child, love,
  was there only as a thing that was not there:
  kinks upon his wrist, his hair, his thigh,
  and other places not so high –
nothing to hold him, no knot even in his mind.

He said, *Ah see ye, king.*
  Ah see yer hanging there silent in yer single knotting.
  And ye could not kill ye!
  Gimme ma fingers but once more,
an' ah'll undo this las', this las' string!

Delusional. He knew not what he spoke of, or to.
I brought him to the only inn I knew would take him.
He snarled no thanks. He snarled,
  no knot now would take him.

A'ave not the fingers fer it. Ah cannot trim them
sharp enough to get between the lines
of this bundle, finer than a flea –
smaller than a mote ah couldn't find.
Trouble 'olds me 'ere on this damn silver beam.

I think he wants to die; I think he's seeking how
      to let go of it all, to cast the anchor off, surrendered
to the wave.
I've seen men flounder so before – he does not know
      that however far often you go down,
      you're alive till you drown.
      Waves at sea are silent, only speaking when
      they break, upon a shore or across a bow,
      and so he endured till the fever flew.

The Drop

Stood upon the bough,
the noose set lightly around my neck,
thought came carried, on a word
as true as flight new-married to a bird,
or blood upon a pulse:

if I were willing to give myself to the drop,
surrendered to its fingers,
putting my back into the fall,
to the sudden crack of its pull,
and at the end be no worse,

in taking all the terror that was offered
by the breeze, of the lunge in the gut,
of the bile caught by the choke
of the slaughtering rope,
and the final, fled darkness,

why should I not, could I not,
give myself instead to the falling of my living years,
however long the drop might be, my neck
subject still undeniably to the break,
just as lost, just as weightless,

perhaps with no hope, but given at least
enough rope...

Itinerant

Every other step on this road pulls
the knot tighter. He walks to the next
place of need, and though the strands
do not impede him, you can see they leave him,
well, stranded – trailing threads snagged.

Practiced fingers picking by firelight
the lines that hold him: some he will keep
as a clean thread, some give to wind. He
will work his shoulders free, offer
salve to the rope-burn, each new morning.

At times he will laugh at himself, beneath
a shady tree, releasing a rabbit from a snare,
its tiny heart running in his hand, sitting
still in fear beside him on the ground;
his own neck taken from the noose willingly.

Loose now, he carries his kindness freely,
but still this lonely knot remains, untied
to anything but itself – were he to offer it
to someone else..? He must walk: there are other
steps needing to be took, others' knots to untighten.

Mr Swarthye

A proper sight we must be together on the road:
I, pale in dusty black; 'im, dark in sun-bleached threads.
'E gets looks as if 'is skin is savage,
though he speaks it like a native.
'I'm on my way to Bath; there's a lady there,
a cook. I met her when in service to Sir–
I hope to marry her; perhaps,
you'll tie the 'trothing rope for me?'
I tie no knots, I reply,
I only loose! And yer've no bindin's on ye,
for me to be of any use.
'I must concur: the strangest thing,
when I first stepped on England's shore,
as the green air pushed aside the salt,
and the gentle hills, still, rolled their hips for me,
like a mother, I felt every bind I had falling free.
    Leaving me just
    with this singleton.'
We'd walked the way together but two days,
when 'e offered up this lonely knot.
I gave 'im mine in return,
and we spent the drawn-out thread of evening
unpickin' each for other.

A Man Called 'Win

...being threads of...

you in your wanderings have untied every bind you have found
i had mine dissolved by the sea, by the being taken to sea
losing the lines of my forebears, the ties to the root of my tongue
i pull on these strings and they come back cut – i have been set
in such freedom upon these shores that no one will see me
no road walked by my fathers – no fire laid by my mothers
what child am i to make, so unfixed? if this woman has me
she too will have had a life of short threads and unreflected
what is left

thread it through. weave it through.

what do you see in dream?   *I see no dream*
  what do you desire?   *No desire*
   what do you need?   *Need's unknotted*
  what to you fear?   *Fear is a lot of loose strings shuffled at my feet*
what do you want

thread it through weave it through

there is a tale of a hanged man
loose on the winds he lies, wi' jus' a noose to 'is ankle to hold him
to a tree – 'e scremmed and pulled down and swung inte every
breeze an' gale, wild in the air an' 'e knew wha' everythin' were –
'e picked up sounds from off the scattered ground an' 'e gan to write
'em down, well, a knotsman cam by, 'eard 'im say, 'fee is the first'

'e loos'd the knot, let 'im drop, said 'fee is fer yer feet now, go do yer
worst!'

thread it through. weave it through

yer a goo' man, 'win Swarthye. Ah sall call ye 'win
as it be the oldest word ah know fer a frien'
and ah will take ye te a wife ah know, wise
in the weavin'. Mebbe, she'l 'ave a braid will int'rest ye

thread it through. weave it through

This line 'ere is yer father's line. I cannot tell you his name, but I can show it you here in this braid, you can feel it in your vein and it shines; this your mother, woven into cloth upon your skin, this the tender grip bore you from the womb into the world, muscles pushing fiercely to shape your face; this your father's father, stout as a weapon grown from the earth, and cut like you,

106

the same scars at the feet; this your father's mother, proud round face of a shining moon, soothed an angry soul; this the mother of your own dear mother, water running, water bearing, holding hands with all that went before, and this the man she chose to make her full, to make her greater still; this his father, short life, left his child alone to find his own kingdom, and mother gone early too, tore herself to see him born; this the father of your father's father…

what do you see in dream?   *I see the world swinging*
what do you desire?   *Desire is a knot I cannot tie*
what do you need?   *A tasty broth would be nice*
what do you fear?   *I fear not fearing*
what do you want?   *I want to meet the hanged man!*

The Hanged Man

                                    – my scrotum lies against my loins,
                   the rest of me, bloodless too, is sunken in, like a snail –
        only, my leg remains straight and rigid, rope burn at the ankle.
             The scream is in my hip, when the wind blows strong –
                                my head is full, like a cock-tip, full and bloody,
                    eye-bulging like one about to spit – too dry to spit,
                               or cry or turn or blink, the rain that collects
              upon my chin will run to the underside of my tongue,
                                    but I have not swallowed since –

Ah cn see he ust to hang by a knotted rope,
but so long ago, th'winds ave carried
all the fronds away
and now he hangs but by a knotted thread
and a black un at that. So long,
that the noose aroun' th'ankle's
burrow'd in, tak'n in
like the livin' wood takes in a nail,
or a bird that died n out of reach.

Approaching him, we were very mindful of the wind, and the emptiness around, how nothing touched him but this one thin strand.

From afar, it seemed he hung, naked, in the very air, and I wondered were the world upside-up and he the only thing not.

The Crow is keeping lightning in his teeth, and storm. I think his eyes can hardly bear to see. Who is this man left hanging? Who is he to him, to me? And how did I even get here?

I fear the answer may be only stony face.

> – I know he thinks to work a knot, disappear it
> into air. I see it in his fingers. I cannot see his eyes –
> The breath of their approach, the two, both black,
> in each their different ways, is sending me
> into inevitable spin, as would deafen me in older days,
> and younger winds – do not touch the cord, I'd have them say.
> So tight, it will take your fingers off; send them dropping
> to the clay –

Cannae see a dog's jaw, is that the clamp upon it?
A knot will show so many haf-truths, time leapin'
from a day's rise to another's night's fall,
and is it a lie b'tween? This line stings
like a nettle-bed, an ah think ah must have a bind
behin' me eyes to make 'em so foggy so...

Crow's gazing at the ankle, held up above his head. He's shown me knots and their unbinding, but for my life, I see no such squirming of lines here. I see only sinew, drawn from out the joint, eased out and lashed around the tree-beam. Has the man hung himself and with himself, left himself dangling like a saggy prick and balls, surrendered to the sky?

The dry, leathery, husk of skin and what remains to be held in, turning slowly in the wind. Or is it he is still, and we and all the world around do turn around around him? I cannot envy his freedom: everything given up, and still he remains tied, always tied, to something.

'I counsel, friend, to leave the string untouched. It has no end, as I can see, the rope and he now indivisible; so too, the rope and tree.'

..nay. There is no knot here.
An' I see nothing but the dead,
swinging like a old spider web
from the branch.

> – the wind of their departure brings me back,
> a louder swing than most – I feel it echo in the motion,
> all the mutual turnings in the woods behind,
> all the branches groaning – 'The web's alive, alive, alive, alive, alive,
> ali –

The Knot Never Tied

There's something of ye makes me want to look away,
it is not thee...
but here's this loose thin rope, see?
trailing from yer, fit to unravel,
such a length of it, there.
Ah know you've carried it all yer life,
my young 'un...
an' ah know it should've been tied.

Ah met a man, a sailor
had a sprog-knot, asked me to unbind it,
save 'im from the hurt of it.
Ah wudnae, because now I was wise.

It's not fer me to tie this now,
'n' I no tier anyhow,
but ah tell ye how I feel,
like the rich woven earth only with all the grown roots
drawn out, left hollow,
left a knotted mat of emptiness
and should-be-there,
dribbled through with rain and worm.
To think I ran when ye were made –
I din't know if it's mine to tie,
p'haps it's yours to decide
have I right?

Walk with me, father.

Across the fields, the starlings
make a murmur, can you feel them?
As if they each were tied to each.
If they were, what a knot they'd make,
would have them crashing to the ground.

Ay, else hanging from the sky…

Strings and stars, they pull us as the earth pulls us,
don't they? As each one pulls the other,
as a child pulls the mother, the father too.
Something to pull against –

They pull on me, I pull on you,
force the word that follows into rhyme,
into something I cannot take for truth
just the ringing of a sound.

Sounds knotted and ne'er to be unbound.

Ay. And I, your rhyme?
Ha! Alright, I can like the sound of that.

I left hanging in the air,
nothing there to chime upon,
just kicking till the swinging's done.
speaking with my father's voice my mother's tongue,
scattered threads spilled as runes across the ground,
a foundling found where?
till you came back…

Found in silence, all of us
bound into the murmur, and I
left with nothing to meet with my rhyme.

Ahh, you, my chil', all this time…

Dad, look. The rope's begun to plait.